LIGHT LUNCHES

Quick and Easy Vegetarian Dishes

LINDA McCARTNEY AND PETER COX

D1494292

BLOOMSBURY

To my husband and children who, like me, love animals and enjoy cooking.

Material taken from *Linda McCartney's Home Cooking*, first published 1989

This special edition produced exclusively for **Today's Vegetarian** 1992
based on *Linda McCartney's Light Lunches* originally published 1992
by Bloomsbury Publishing Limited
2 Soho Square, London W1V 5DE

The moral right of the authors has been asserted.

A copy of the CIP entry for this book is available from the British Library.

Designed by Fielding Rowinski
Typeset by Columns of Reading
Printed in England by Clays Ltd, St Ives Plc

CONTENTS

Introduction iv

1. Hot dishes 1

2. Cold dishes 40

3. Salads, Dips and Pâtés 46

4. Soups and Bread 66

Index 90

INTRODUCTION

I was lucky enough to grow up in a family of food lovers. We rarel had fancy meals but they always tasted good. I used to spend a lot c time hanging out in the kitchen, partly because I liked to be aroun food, but also because I loved to watch my mum preparing a meal ofte without measuring or weighing any ingredients. She just seemed t know instinctively what was right.

I like to think I'm a person who picks things up easily and thos hours I spent hanging around the kitchen have served me well They've given me a natural feeling for putting together a meal withou spending hours poring over recipes.

There is, of course, one main difference between my cooking and th food I was brought up on – I don't use any meat but everybody seem to say it tastes as good as, if not better than using (to put it bluntly dead animals.

Which brings me to the reason I've written this book. Partly as a wa of handing down my recipes to my family, but most importantl because I want to encourage all those people who so often say to me 'I'd like to cook without using meat but I don't know where to begin' or 'How do you fill that gap on the plate where there's usually a piec of lamb or beef?' My response is simple – there are quiches, pastas salads and many wonderful new soya protein foods that taste so muc better than meat!

And to those people who complain: 'I'd love to be a vegetarian bu my family would never allow it', I suggest you try a few of my recipes without mentioning there's no meat – and see how much they enjo them!

We stopped eating meat many years ago. During the course of a Sunday lunch we happened to look out of the kitchen window at our young lambs gambolling happily in the fields. Glancing down at our plates we suddenly realized that we were eating the leg of an animal that had until recently been gambolling in a field itself. We looked at each other and said 'Wait a minute, we love these sheep – they're such gentle creatures, so why are we eating them?' It was the last time we ever did.

Some people find it easier to cut out meat gradually, supplementing their diet with chicken and fish. We chose not to take this route – a decision which was reinforced a few weeks later when we found ourselves stuck behind a truck packed tightly with beautiful white hens. As it turned into the chicken processing plant a few miles ahead, we imagined the fate in store for those poor hens and felt we had acted wisely.

There are people who try to justify eating fish by saying they have no feelings. Well, you watch a fish gasping for breath as it's pulled out of the water and then try and tell me it has no feelings! Anyway, with the amount of pollution in our poisoned rivers and seas, I'm surprised that *anyone* wants to eat fish. But that's another story. . .

I think a lot of people are rather afraid of cooking. I've met so many people who say: 'Oh, I could never cook that!' when more often than not it's just been a bunch of really good food thrown together – and doesn't it taste good! It's a shame that so many people shy away from the kitchen because it can be an artistic and creative place. And rewarding too – it's great to prepare a meal that is well received.

I don't think you have to be a particularly talented person to be a good cook. It helps enormously, of course, if you enjoy cooking, but even if you don't I hope this book will encourage you to have a go – and maybe you'll find you start to get some unexpected pleasure out of it!

To tell you the truth, I'm a real peasant cook. My cooking has never been about following recipes in a book, and it's been a challenge to translate these instinctive methods into hard and fast rules. For example, if I'm making a stew I *never* weigh the carrots, potatoes, and onions. I simply say: 'that looks the right amount' and in they go. If you like a particular herb, or if you like garlic, onions or potatoes, then add more of what you like to my recipes – don't be afraid to make a few changes to suit your own taste. That's what cooking's all about!

The important thing, I believe, is to have a really good time cooking. Don't be too serious, and – most of all – don't be 'precious'.

I spend a lot of time in our kitchen. I find it the cosiest, friendliest place in the house. It's not something my American upbringing prepared me for, but now that I live in England it's become very important to me. It's a great place to nurture a happy harmonious family and to spend time with friends, chatting over a cup of tea.

I've put down a lot of my favourite recipes here and I really hope you find them as easy to make as I do. They're very popular with everybody I know, and I hope they'll become favourites of yours as well. I haven't written this book in order to be acclaimed as a great cook – like everyone, I've had my share of disasters in the kitchen. I'm simply doing it for the animals.

Linda McCartney

HOT DISHES

Aubergine Fritters

This recipe should produce about 10 fritters. Serve hot with a selection of steamed vegetables or salads.

1 aubergine
2oz/55g plain flour
1 teaspoon baking powder
1–2 tablespoons chopped fresh herbs
salt and freshly ground black pepper to taste
2 tablespoons milk
1 egg
oil for frying

Cover the aubergine with boiling water and cook for 15 minutes. Slice the hot aubergine in half, scoop out the seeds and discard. Spoon the flesh into a bowl and mash with a fork.

Mix the flour, baking powder, herbs, salt and pepper together in a bowl. Stir well.

Whisk the milk and egg together in a jug. Make a well in the dry ingredients and gradually add this liquid, stirring well after each addition. Finally, add the mashed aubergine and work into a thick paste.

Drop spoonsful of the paste into hot oil and fry until light brown, drain and serve immediately.

40 minutes to make

Baked and Creamed Sweet Potatoes

For a quick and tasty snack, serve with salad or a green vegetable. Alternatively, serve with other vegetables as an accompaniment to a main course.

4 medium sweet potatoes
1oz/25g butter or margarine
salt and freshly ground black pepper to taste

Pre-heat the oven to 375°F/190°C (Gas Mark 5). Wash the sweet potatoes and bake them for about 45–60 minutes until they are tender.

Peel the potatoes and mash them in a bowl with the butter, salt and pepper. Whip them to a smooth puree. Serve immediately.

1 hour 10 minutes to make
Good source of vitamin A, vitamin C

Baked Steaklets

The 'steaklets' I'm talking about here are made from TVP. In fact you can use any similar TVP product, such as vegetable burgers, sausages or frankfurters. While you can make them up from packet mixes, it is probably easier to buy them ready made – either from the freezer department in supermarkets, or in cans from health food shops. Serve with rice or potatoes, and green vegetables or a salad.

1½oz/45g butter or margarine
1 large onion, chopped
1lb/455g mushrooms, sliced
6 vegetable burgers or steaklets
2 cloves garlic, crushed or 1 teaspoon garlic powder
8fl.oz/230ml tomato ketchup

Pre-heat the oven to 400°F/200°C (Gas Mark 6) and lightly grease a casserole dish.

Melt half the butter in a frying pan. Sauté the onion until lightly browned, then remove and place to one side. Sauté the mushrooms in the same butter until light brown, then remove, keeping separate from the onions.

Heat the remaining butter in the frying pan and brown the burgers – about 5 minutes in total. Remove from the heat and sprinkle both sides with garlic. Place the burgers in the casserole dish.

Cover the burgers with the onions, spreading them to the edges of the dish. Now pour the ketchup over the onions and spread it evenly also. Finally, top the dish with the sautéd mushrooms. Cover the dish and bake for 30 minutes. Serve immediately.

45 minutes to make
Good source of protein, B group vitamins, potassium

Bean Tacos

You can find taco shells in most supermarkets these days – Mexican food is increasingly popular, because it's both tasty and quick to make.

for the taco sauce:
2 medium onions
1 × 4oz/115g tin green chillies in brine
4 large tomatoes
juice of ½ lemon

to serve:
2 tablespoons olive oil
1 × 14oz/397g tin refried beans
6oz/170g Cheddar cheese, grated
6 taco shells
1 iceberg or Webb's lettuce, shredded

Pre-heat the oven to 325°F/170°C (Gas Mark 3).

To make the sauce – finely chop the onions, drain and finely chop the chillies. Peel and chop the tomatoes, then mix the onions, chillies and tomatoes with the lemon juice in a mixing bowl.

Heat the oil in a pan, add the beans and cook gently for 4–5 minutes, then mash roughly with a fork. Place the taco shells in the oven until they are warm – approximately 3 minutes.

Spoon the beans into the hot taco shells. Top with the lettuce, grated cheese, and a spoonful of sauce. Serve immediately.

20 minutes to make
Good source of protein, vitamin A, B group vitamins, vitamin C

Beer Rarebit

This is very good accompanied with a salad or a vegetable speciality such as Green Bean Savoury.

2oz/55g butter or margarine
8oz/225g Cheddar cheese, grated
4 tablespoons beer
1 tablespoon mild mustard
½ teaspoon paprika
salt and freshly ground black pepper to taste
1 teaspoon Worcestershire sauce

to serve:
rice or toast

Melt the butter in a deep saucepan, then add the remaining ingredients. Stir well, over a gentle heat, until the cheese has melted. Pour over rice or toast, and serve immediately.

15 minutes to make
Good source of protein, vitamin A, calcium

Burger Goulash

Serve with rice or mashed potatoes, and green vegetables or a salad.

1oz/25g butter or margarine
1 large onion, chopped
1 clove garlic, crushed
6 vegetable burgers, cubed
1oz/30g plain flour
1 tablespoon paprika
1 × 14oz/397g tin chopped tomatoes
5fl.oz/140ml red wine
8 small new potatoes or 2 large baking potatoes, cubed
salt and freshly ground black pepper to taste
5fl.oz/140ml sour cream (optional)

Melt the butter in a pan and fry the onion and garlic for 4–5 minutes. Coat the burger chunks in flour, then add them to the pan and brown gently. Add the paprika, tomatoes, wine and potatoes. Season to taste.

Cover the goulash and simmer gently for about 25 minutes.

Just before serving, stir in the sour cream and sprinkle a little extra paprika over the dish to garnish.

45 minutes to make
Good source of vitamin A, B group vitamins, vitamin C, potassium

Burgers à la King

Serve hot over rice or crispy noodles, or as a vol-au-vent filling. Great with green vegetables or salads.

for the white sauce:
2oz/55g butter or margarine
1oz/25g plain flour
15fl.oz/430ml milk

for the rest of the recipe:
1oz/25g butter or margarine
1 medium onion, chopped
4 vegetable burgers, cubed
8 oz/225g button mushrooms, chopped
½ green pepper, chopped
2 teaspoons paprika
8fl.oz/230ml vegetable stock or water
4 tablespoons sherry
2 egg yolks, beaten
salt and freshly ground black pepper to taste

Prepare a white sauce with the butter, flour and milk and keep it warm over a very low heat.

Melt the butter in a small saucepan and sauté the onion in it for 4–5 minutes until lightly browned.

Add the burger chunks to the pan and lightly brown – about 5 minutes in total.

Add the mushrooms, green pepper and paprika, then pour in the white sauce, vegetable stock and sherry. Simmer, covered, for 15 minutes. Stir in the egg yolks, salt and pepper and cook for a further 2 minutes. Serve immediately.

30 minutes to make
Good source of protein, vitamin A, B group vitamins, vitamin C

Burgers Chop Suey

Serve with rice or noodles and any vegetable.

   3 tablespoons vegetable oil
   6 vegetable burgers
   1 clove garlic, crushed
   2 medium onions, chopped
   8oz/225g mushrooms, sliced
   4 sticks celery, chopped
   4oz/115g water chestnuts, thinly sliced
   4oz /115g beansprouts
   2 tablespoons cornflour
   1 tablespoon sherry
   2 tablespoons soy sauce
   up to ½ pint/290ml vegetable stock

Pre-heat the oven to 350°F/180°C (Gas Mark 4). Heat 1 tablespoon of the oil in a frying pan and brown the burgers on both sides, about 5 minutes in total. Remove them from the pan and place to one side.

Sauté the garlic and onions in the remaining oil until they just begin to soften. Add the mushrooms, celery and water chestnuts and sauté for 10 minutes. Add the beansprouts and cook for a further 5 minutes.

Mix the cornflour, sherry, soy sauce and stock together in a large jug. Add this liquid to the sauté and stir gently until it thickens into a sauce. Cook for a further 10 minutes.

Put the burgers in the bottom of a large casserole, cover with the sauce and bake, uncovered, for 20 minutes. Stir gently before serving.

55 minutes to make
Good source of B group vitamins, vitamin C

Cauliflower Gratin

1 large cauliflower
1 tablespoon olive oil
1 large onion, chopped
4oz/115g raisins
2oz/55g pine nuts
1oz/25g Parmesan cheese, grated

Cut the cauliflower into florets and steam for about 10 minutes, until it is just tender.

Heat the oil in a large frying pan and sauté the onion. Add the raisins and pine nuts, and continue the sauté. Add the steamed cauliflower and mix well.

Spoon the mixture into a wide casserole dish and top with the grated Parmesan. Put under a medium grill for 5 minutes, until the cheese has browned. Serve hot.

20 minutes to make
Good source of protein, B group vitamins, vitamin C, calcium

Cheddar Cheese Balls

Makes 8 small balls, enough to serve as an appetizer for 4 people.

1oz/25g plain flour
4oz/115g Cheddar cheese, grated
salt and freshly ground black pepper to taste
1 egg white
oil for frying

Mix the flour, cheese, salt and pepper in a bowl. In another bowl, beat the egg white until firm. Fold the flour and cheese mixture into the beaten egg white.

Shape this mixture into little balls and drop into very hot oil. Fry until golden brown, then serve immediately.

15 minutes to make
Good source of calcium

Corn Fritters

Great with a green salad.

8oz/225g sweetcorn or 2 medium ears sweetcorn, trimmed
1 egg
7fl.oz/205ml milk
4oz/115g plain flour
½ teaspoon salt
freshly ground black pepper to taste
vegetable oil for frying

Cook the corn until it is tender, and drain well.

To make the batter, beat the egg and milk together. Then add the flour, salt and pepper and blend until smooth.

Stir the corn into the batter. Drop spoonsful into very hot oil, and fry on both sides until lightly browned.

Drain on paper towels to remove excess oil, and serve immediately.

25 minutes to make
Good source of B group vitamins

Cream of Celery

Serve this over pasta or beside fresh garden peas and baby carrots.

2oz/55g butter or margarine
8 large sticks celery, sliced
2 tablespoons finely chopped onion or 1 small onion, finely chopped
2 tablespoons plain flour
6fl.oz/180ml vegetable stock or water
4fl.oz/120ml single cream

Melt the butter in a saucepan over a very low heat. Add the celery and onion and stir well to coat. Cover the pan and leave over the heat, without stirring, for 15 minutes. Shake the pan occasionally if necessary, as the butter must not burn.

Uncover the saucepan and sprinkle the flour over the vegetables. Stir well, then gradually add the vegetable stock and the cream.

Stir constantly until the mixture comes to a boil. Reduce the heat and simmer, uncovered, until the sauce has thickened. Serve hot.

25 minutes to make
Good source of vitamin A

Courgettes with Apples

1½lb/680g small courgettes, thinly sliced
2oz/55g butter or margarine
1 medium onion, chopped
2 eating apples, chopped
2 fresh tomatoes, peeled and chopped
2 tablespoons chopped fresh parsley
salt and freshly ground black pepper to taste

Set a small pan of water to boil. Drop the courgette slices into the boiling water for 30 seconds. Remove immediately and drain.

Melt the butter in a frying pan and sauté the onion until it is transparent. Add the apples and stir well to coat with the butter. Add the tomatoes and the blanched courgettes. Stir well, then add the parsley.

Season this mixture and leave it to cook, covered, over a gentle heat for 5–10 minutes, until the courgettes are soft. Serve hot.

35 minutes to make
Good source of vitamin A, vitamin C

Fried Mozzarella

Serve hot with a tomato sauce.

1lb/455g Mozzarella cheese
1 egg
2oz/55g plain flour
1oz/25g breadcrumbs
oil for frying

Cut the cheese into 2¾ inch/7cm squares, approximately 1 inch/2.5cm thick.

Break the egg into a small bowl and beat it well. Measure the flour into a second bowl and the breadcrumbs into a third bowl.

Dredge the cheese squares in flour, then dip them into the beaten egg. Immediately dip them in breadcrumbs, then the egg again, then the bread-crumbs again.

Fry the cheese squares in the oil until they are golden. Drain before serving.

15 minutes to make
Good source of protein, vitamin A, calcium

French Fried Vegetables

1lb/455g mixed fresh vegetables
6oz/170g plain flour
pinch of salt
1 egg, beaten
8fl.oz/230ml milk
oil for frying

Cut the vegetables into bite-sized pieces and parboil or steam them until they are half-cooked. Drain the vegetables, dry them on a tea towel and put to one side.

Measure the flour into a bowl. Drop the egg into the centre of the flour and begin to stir them together. Gradually add the milk to the egg and flour and stir constantly to make a smooth batter.

Dip the dry vegetable pieces into this batter, drop into very hot oil and fry until golden brown.

Drain the fried vegetables on a paper towel and serve immediately with a light sprinkling of salt.

15 minutes to make

Green Beans and Mushrooms in Sour Cream

Sour cream can sometimes curdle during cooking, which won't spoil the taste but may not be so appealing to look at. To stop this happening, mix a teaspoon of cornflour into the sour cream before adding it to the vegetables.

8oz/225g French beans
1½oz/45g butter or margarine
8oz/225g mushrooms, chopped
4fl.oz/120ml sour cream
salt and freshly ground black pepper to taste

Steam the beans until just tender. Set them aside to drain well.

Melt the butter in a large pan and sauté the mushrooms until they are quite tender. Keep the heat quite high so they do not release their juice.

Stir in the cooked beans and heat them through, then add the sour cream and seasoning.

Cook briefly, without boiling, until the beans are quite hot. Serve immediately.

20 minutes to make
Good source of protein, B group vitamins, potassium

Green Bean Savoury

Serve with rice or quiche.

1½lb/680g green beans
2 tablespoons vegetable oil
1 small onion, finely chopped
1 clove garlic, crushed
2 sticks celery, chopped
2 carrots, shredded
1 teaspoon dried basil or 1 tablespoon chopped fresh basil
salt and freshly ground black pepper to taste
4 tablespoons vegetable stock or water
2oz/55g Parmesan cheese, grated

Steam the beans until just tender. Heat the oil in a frying pan and sauté the chopped onion and garlic, stirring constantly.

Add the celery and carrot and sauté for 3–4 minutes, stirring often.

Add the cooked beans, basil, salt and pepper. Pour in a little stock if necessary if the contents of the pan seem dry. Cover the pan and simmer over a low heat for 5 minutes.

Remove the pan from the heat and stir in half the Parmesan cheese. Pour the savoury into a warmed serving dish, top with the remaining cheese and serve immediately.

25 minutes to make
Good source of vitamin A, vitamin C, calcium, iron

Leeks Vinaigrette

Serve with rice, salad, baked potatoes or as a starter. For an interesting variation, try adding 2 tablespoons pickles or capers.

2lb/910g leeks
1 teaspoon mild mustard
2 cloves garlic, crushed
1 tablespoon lemon juice
1 tablespoon vinegar
4 tablespoons olive oil
salt and freshly ground black pepper to taste
2oz/55g olives

Wash, trim and steam the leeks until tender. Then slice them in half lengthways and arrange in a serving dish.

Mix the mustard and garlic with the lemon juice, vinegar and olive oil and season to taste.

Chop the olives and stir them into the dressing. Pour over the hot leeks and serve immediately.

15 minutes to make
Good source of vitamin C, B group vitamins, iron

Hot Mozzarella Sandwich

Serve hot with a salad.

8 slices wholemeal bread
8 thin slices Mozzarella cheese
2 eggs, beaten
5fl.oz/140ml milk
1oz/25g plain flour
enough olive oil or vegetable oil to cover the bottom of a frying pan

Trim the crusts from the slices of bread. Make 4 closed sandwiches, using two slices of cheese per sandwich. Heat the oil in the frying pan until it is hot but not smoking.

Mix the beaten eggs with the milk. Measure the flour onto a plate.

Brush a little of the egg mixture around the edges of each sandwich so that it holds together. Then dip each sandwich completely, but quickly, into the egg-and-milk mixture. Lift the sandwich out of the egg, on to the plate and lightly coat both sides with flour.

Fry the sandwiches in the hot oil for 3–4 minutes each side, or until lightly browned. When the cheese starts to melt, remove the sandwich from the pan. Place in a warm oven or under a grill until all 4 sandwiches are ready, then serve immediately.

25 minutes to make
Good source of protein, B group vitamins, calcium

Meatless Balls

Serve with vegetables or as part of another recipe.

1lb/455g vegetable burgers
½oz/15g breadcrumbs
salt and freshly ground black pepper to taste
1oz/25g butter or margarine
1 large onion, chopped
5fl.oz/140ml milk
1 egg, beaten
1 tablespoon chopped fresh parsley
1 tablespoon soy sauce
vegetable oil for frying

Crumble the burgers into a mixing bowl and use your fingers to work in the breadcrumbs, salt and pepper. Set to one side.

Melt the butter in a frying pan and sauté the onion until transparent.

Mix the milk and egg together and add, with the parsley and soy sauce, to the dry mix. Stir well, then add the onion sauté also. Stir this mixture thoroughly, and shape into 24 small balls.

Fry the meatless balls until well browned all over. Serve immediately.

1 hour to make
Good source of protein

Mexican Rarebit

Serve over toast, rice or baked potato.

1½oz/45g butter or margarine
1 small onion, chopped
1 × 4oz/115g tin green chillies in brine, drained and chopped
2 tablespoons plain flour
8fl.oz/230ml milk
5oz/140g Cheddar cheese, grated
1 × 14oz/397g tin chopped tomatoes, drained
salt and freshly ground black pepper to taste

Melt the butter in a saucepan and sauté the onion. Add the chillies and stir well.

Sprinkle the flour over the sauté and stir well to make a thick paste. Gradually add the milk, stirring constantly, to make a smooth sauce.

Add the cheese, tomatoes, salt and pepper and stir well. Serve immediately.

15 minutes to make
Good source of protein, vitamin A, B group vitamins, vitamin C

Mexican Omelette

2 large eggs
1 × 4oz/115g tin green chillies in brine, drained and chopped
1 teaspoon butter or margarine
salt and freshly ground black pepper to taste

Drain and chop the chillies. Whisk the egg in a mixing bowl and add the chopped green chillies.

Heat the butter in the frying pan, pour in the egg mixture, season with salt and pepper and cook for 1–2 minutes over a high heat.

Keeping the omelette over the heat, use a spatula to fold it over. Slide it out of the pan on to a warm plate. Serve piping hot.

10 minutes to make
Good source of vitamin A, vitamin C

Mozzarella Croquettes

Serve with a selection of green vegetables, and top with home-made tomato sauce.

12oz/340g plain flour
salt and freshly ground black pepper to taste
2 eggs
1lb/455g Mozzarella cheese, grated
2oz/55g fresh breadcrumbs
vegetable oil for frying

for the garnish:
1 tablespoon chopped fresh parsley

Mix the flour, salt and pepper together in a mixing bowl.

Break the eggs into the centre of the flour mixture and stir in ever-increasing circles. When a doughy consistency is reached, add the grated Mozzarella and keep stirring.

Shape this mixture into balls or croquettes and roll them in the breadcrumbs until they are well coated.

Deep-fry until the croquettes are a golden brown. Serve hot with a sprinkling of parsley.

15 minutes to make
Good source of protein, vitamin A, B group vitamins, calcium

Mozzarella French Loaf

1 medium stick French bread
1lb/455g Mozzarella cheese, sliced
1oz/25g butter or margarine, melted
2 cloves garlic, chopped
1 teaspoon chopped fresh oregano

Pre-heat the oven to 425°F/220°C (Gas Mark 7). Make diagonal cuts into the French loaf all the way along its length, at ½ inch/1–2cm intervals, but without slicing it all the way through. Place the loaf on a baking tray.

Push a slice of Mozzarella into each cut. Brush the melted butter over the loaf, and sprinkle the garlic and oregano over all.

Bake for 10–15 minutes until the crust is lightly browned and the cheese is bubbly.

20 minutes to make
Good source of protein, vitamin A, calcium

New Orleans Okra

Serve hot over rice or toast.

2 tablespoons olive oil
1 medium onion, chopped
1 small red or green or yellow pepper, chopped
12oz/340g okra (sometimes called ladies' fingers), sliced
1 × 14oz/397g tin chopped tomatoes
1 tablespoon chopped fresh basil or 1 teaspoon dried basil
salt and freshly ground black pepper to taste

Heat the oil in a saucepan and sauté the onion and pepper gently for 5–6 minutes, until lightly browned.

Increase the heat, add the okra and sauté for 5 minutes, stirring constantly.

Reduce the heat and add the tomatoes, herb and seasoning. Stir well, cover the pan and simmer for 15 minutes. Add more liquid, such as tomato juice or vegetable stock, if desired.

30 minutes to make
Good source of vitamin A, vitamin C, calcium

Niçoise Green Beans

Try serving with rice, mashed potatoes or potato pancakes.

  2 tablespoons olive oil
  1 medium onion, chopped
  2 sticks celery, chopped
  1lb/455g French green beans
  1 × 14oz/397g tin chopped tomatoes
  4 tablespoons vegetable stock or tomato juice
  1 bay leaf
  ½oz/15g fresh parsley, chopped
  salt and freshly ground black pepper to taste

Heat the oil in a large frying pan and gently sauté the onions and celery until lightly browned.

Boil or steam the French beans until tender (about 10 minutes). Drain and set aside.

Add the tomatoes, stock, bay leaf and parsley to the sauté. Stir well and simmer this sauce for 20 minutes, uncovered. Season to taste.

Add the cooked beans to the sauce and stir well. Bring back to a simmer and cook for a further 2 minutes. Serve immediately.

35 minutes to make
Good source of vitamin A, vitamin C

Noodles and Garlic

8oz/225g pasta noodles
6 tablespoons olive oil
3 cloves garlic, finely chopped

to serve:
2oz/55g Parmesan cheese, grated

Cook the noodles in a large saucepan of boiling, salted water for about 12–15 minutes, until tender. Rinse under cold water, drain and return them to the saucepan.

Heat the oil in a small saucepan and sauté the garlic very gently for 2–3 minutes until slightly crisp. Toss the oil and garlic in with the cooked pasta and sprinkle with Parmesan cheese. Serve immediately.

20 minutes to make
Good source of calcium

Noodles German Style

8oz/225g pasta noodles
2oz/55g butter or margarine
1lb/455g mushrooms, sliced
4 tablespoons chopped fresh parsley
1oz/25g breadcrumbs

Cook the noodles in a large saucepan of boiling, salted water until just tender. Rinse under cold water and drain.

Melt the butter in a frying pan and sauté the mushrooms until lightly browned.

Add the cooked noodles, parsley and breadcrumbs, mix thoroughly and serve immediately.

25 minutes to make
Good source of vitamin A, B group vitamins

Omelette

This simple recipe is the basis for countless variations according to your individual taste. Serves 1 person.

2 eggs
salt and freshly ground black pepper to taste
½oz/15g butter or margarine
filling of your choice (grated cheese, hot chopped fried onion, hot cooked spinach etc)

Beat the eggs together in a mixing bowl until they froth. Season to taste.

Melt the butter in a 6 inch/18cm frying pan and keep it over a medium to high heat. Pour the eggs into the hot pan and leave it undisturbed while it cooks.

When the upper surface begins to bubble, lift the cooked edges and allow the uncooked egg to run underneath. When lightly browned underneath, flip it over like a pancake and lightly brown it on the other side.

Remove the omelette from the pan with the help of a spatula, and turn it on to a hot dish. Fold it in half if it is to be eaten plain; otherwise place the filling (cheese, onion, spinach, fried chopped mushrooms, etc) on one half and fold the other half of the omelette over it. Serve immediately.

minutes to make

Pasta with Herbs

1lb/455g noodles (spaghetti or macaroni)
3 tablespoons chopped fresh parsley
3 tablespoons chopped fresh basil
1 tablespoon chopped fresh oregano
1 clove garlic, crushed
3fl.oz/90ml olive oil
8oz/225g cottage cheese

Cook the pasta until tender, rinse under cold water and drain.

Mix the herbs, garlic, oil and cheese in a blender, and liquidize to make a sauce.

Add the sauce to the cooked pasta and gently heat, while stirring. Serve immediately.

25 minutes to make
Good source of protein, vitamin A, calcium, iron

asties

A meal in themselves, especially with a nice green salad.

2 medium potatoes
12oz/340g shortcrust pastry
2 medium onions
1oz/25g butter or margarine
half a 4½oz/128g packet TVP mince or 4 vegetable burgers, crumbled
salt and freshly ground black pepper to taste

Pre-heat the oven to 350°F/180°C (Gas Mark 4). Cut the potatoes into cubes and parboil for 5 minutes, until slightly tender but not soft.

Roll out the pastry into a number of 9 inch/23cm rounds and set aside.

Chop the onions and sauté them in the butter in a frying pan until light brown. Add the potatoes and the crumbled vegetable burgers to the sauté and cook for 5 minutes, stirring frequently.

Spoon the mixture into the centre of one half of each round of pastry. Sprinkle a little salt and pepper over the stuffing, then fold the pastry over the filling and press the edges together using a fork.

Cut one or two small slashes in each pasty and bake on a greased baking sheet for 45 minutes until lightly golden in colour.

hour to make
Good source of protein

Peas in Cream

12oz/340g peas, frozen or fresh
2oz/55g butter or margarine
3–4 spring onions, chopped
4 sticks celery, chopped
4fl.oz/120ml cream
2 tablespoons chopped fresh tarragon
salt and freshly ground black pepper to taste

Cook the peas. Melt the butter and sauté the onions and celery until just tender. Add the cooked peas to the sauté.

Stir in the cream and tarragon. Cook for 5 minutes, uncovered, over very low heat. Season to taste. Serve immediately.

20 minutes to make
Good source of vitamin A, B group vitamins, vitamin C, calcium

Potato Dumplings with Brown Butter

These quantities should make 12 dumplings.

4 large potatoes, cubed
1 egg, beaten
6oz/170g self-raising flour
salt and freshly ground black pepper to taste
2oz/55g butter
2oz/55g dried breadcrumbs

Boil the potatoes until tender, then mash them and allow to cool.

Add the egg, flour, salt and pepper to the potatoes and mix well using your hands. Shape the mixture into little balls (about ping-pong size).

Drop the dumplings into boiling water and cook gently for 1 minutes. Heat the butter in a pan and allow to brown for a couple c minutes, then mix with the breadcrumbs in a separate bowl.

Remove the dumplings from the water and drain them on a pape towel. Serve immediately with a sprinkling of the breadcrumb mixture

40 minutes to make
Good source of B group vitamins

Ratatouille

Use good-quality olive oil in this recipe, and be careful not to stir the dish too vigorously because it will break up the vegetables. Instead, use a wooden spatula and lift, like tossing a salad, to preserve the texture of each vegetable.

 2lb/910g whole tomatoes
 1 medium (8oz/225g) aubergine
 4 tablespoons olive oil
 1 large courgette, sliced
 2 medium onions, chopped
 1 large green pepper, deseeded and sliced
 8oz/225g mushrooms, sliced
 2–3 cloves garlic, crushed
 1 tablespoon chopped fresh parsley
 salt and freshly ground black pepper to taste

 for the garnish:
 2 tablespoons capers
 1 lemon, cut into wedges

Plunge the tomatoes into boiling water for 1 minute. Remove them, then cut out the cores and peel them. Slice them in half and remove the pulp and seeds. Then turn the tomato shells on to a paper towel and leave to drain.

Peel and slice the aubergine. Pour the olive oil into a large, deep pan and place over a medium flame. Sauté the aubergine and courgette slices for 1–2 minutes until they are lightly browned. Remove them from the oil and drain on paper towels.

Use the same oil to sauté the onions, green pepper, mushrooms and garlic for about 10 minutes over a low heat, stirring frequently.

Place the aubergine and courgette slices over this sauté and sprinkle with the parsley. Top with the tomato shells, cover the pan and cook over a low heat for 15 minutes. Remove the lid and continue cooking for 1 hour, until the mixture is thick and most of the liquid is gone. Season to taste.

Serve hot or cold with a garnish of capers and lemon wedges.

1 hour 45 minutes to make
Good source of vitamin A, B group vitamins, vitamin C

Sauerkraut and Veggy Dogs

Great with mashed potatoes, boiled potatoes or potato pancakes, and a touch of apple sauce.

2 tablespoons vegetable oil
1 medium onion, sliced
salt and freshly ground black pepper to taste
2 pints/1.1l sauerkraut
6 vegetable sausages
1 teaspoon caraway seeds
5fl.oz/140ml water

Heat the oil and sauté the onion until tender. Stir in the salt and pepper and add this mixture to the sauerkraut in a large saucepan.

Add the uncooked sausages and the caraway seeds and stir gently. Add the water, cover the pan and simmer for 15–20 minutes.

Alternatively, pre-heat the oven to 350°F/180°C (Gas Mark 4) and pour the mixture into a greased casserole dish. Bake, covered, for 30 minutes, adding extra water if necessary towards the end of the cooking time.

40 minutes to make
Good source of vitamin C, iron

Sausage Rolls

A great quick lunch, served with a salad.

6oz/170g puff pastry
8 vegetable sausages (about 3 inches/7.5cm long), cooked
1 egg, beaten

Pre-heat the oven to 425°F/220°C (Gas Mark 7). Roll the puff pastry into a thin rectangle 24 × 5 inches/ 60 × 12.5cm and cut into 8 long, thin strips, 3 × 5 inches/7.5 × 12.5cm. This can be varied according to the size of the sausage.

Place a sausage across the centre of each strip of pastry and wrap the pastry round the sausage, pinching the ends of the pastry together with a moist fork.

Cut the prepared sausage rolls in half and brush the pastry with the beaten egg.

Bake for 15–20 minutes on a greased baking tray. Cool on a wire rack, or serve immediately.

40 minutes to make

Simple Stuffed Mushrooms

8 large mushrooms
2 tablespoons vegetable oil
4oz/115g breadcrumbs
4 tablespoons chopped fresh parsley
2 cloves garlic, crushed
1 egg, beaten
salt and freshly ground black pepper to taste

Pre-heat the oven to 350°F/180°C (Gas Mark 4) (alternatively, you can use the grill). Remove the stems from the mushrooms. Brush the mushroom tops with a little oil. Scoop out some of the mushroom centres and chop finely with the stems.

Mix the remaining ingredients together in a bowl and add the chopped mushroom stems. Season to taste.

Divide this filling between the mushroom tops, then brush with a little more oil.

Place the stuffed mushrooms on a greased baking dish and bake for 10–15 minutes, or place the tray under a hot grill for 10 minutes. Serve immediately.

25 minutes to make
Good source of vitamin A, B group vitamins, vitamin C

Sloppy Joes

Serve hot over muffins, in toasted baps or over rice with green salad.
Serves 2.

1 medium onion, chopped
1oz/25g butter or margarine
4 vegetable burgers
1 small red or green or yellow pepper, sliced (optional)
2oz/55g mushrooms, sliced
4 tablespoons tomato ketchup
salt and freshly ground black pepper to taste

Sauté the onion in the butter until light brown. Crumble the burgers
and add them to the sauté, stirring often.
  Add the sliced pepper and mushrooms and continue stirring.
  Add the ketchup, salt and pepper and cook the mixture, uncovered,
for 5 minutes, stirring occasionally.

20 minutes to make
Good source of protein, vitamin C

Stuffed and Broiled Mushrooms

'Broiling' simply means 'grilling'. Try serving with a good-sized salad

9–12 very large mushrooms
2 tablespoons vegetable oil or olive oil
1 medium onion, chopped
1 clove garlic, crushed (optional)
1 × 4½oz/128g packet TVP mince
2oz/55g fresh breadcrumbs
2 tablespoons cream
1 teaspoon sherry
5fl.oz/140ml vegetable stock
salt and freshly ground black pepper to taste

Pre-heat the oven to 350°F/180°c (Gas Mark 4). Clean the mushrooms and remove their stems. Chop the stems finely and place the mushroom caps bottom-up on a lightly-oiled baking tray. Brush the mushrooms with a little oil, cover the tray and bake for 10–15 minutes.

Heat the oil in a frying pan and sauté the onion and garlic until soft. Add the chopped mushroom stems and the TVP mince. Stir well and continue to sauté the mixture for 4–5 minutes.

Add the rest of the ingredients, stir and cook for a further 4–5 minutes.

Spoon a little of the mixture into each of the mushrooms in the baking tray. Cook under the grill for about 5 minutes. Serve immediately.

35 minutes to make
Good source of protein

Tarragon and Herb Eggs

Rice or salad is an excellent accompaniment to this very tasty dish.

7fl.oz/205ml milk
7fl.oz/205ml single cream
4 eggs, beaten
2 tablespoons chopped fresh tarragon
1 tablespoon chopped fresh parsley or any fresh herb combination of your choice
salt and freshly ground black pepper to taste

for the garnish:
chopped fresh parsley

Pre-heat the oven to 350°F/180°C (Gas Mark 4) and lightly grease 4 individual custard cups or ramekins. Place the cups in a baking tray filled with water. Mix the milk and cream together in a saucepan and heat to just below boiling point.

Add the hot milk mixture to the eggs, stirring constantly. As you stir, add the herbs, salt and pepper.

Pour the egg mixture into the ramekins, filling each about three-quarters full. Bake them in the tray of water for 20 minutes (the water surround ensures they do not cook too fast).

Then insert a piece of raw spaghetti into the contents of one of the ramekins. If the eggs are cooked, the spaghetti will come out clean. Serve hot with a garnish of fresh parsley.

30 minutes to make
Good source of vitamin A, calcium, iron

Quiche

6oz/170g shortcrust pastry
1oz/25g butter or margarine
1 large onion, chopped
4 eggs, beaten
15fl.oz/430ml milk
5fl.oz/140ml cream
10oz/285g Cheddar or Swiss cheese, grated
salt and freshly ground black pepper to taste

Pre-heat the oven to 400°F/200°C (Gas Mark 6). Grease your quiche dish, roll out the pastry and press it round the bottom and sides of the dish. Place some greaseproof paper filled with baking beans or dry rice on the pastry, and bake it blind for about 10 minutes, until the pastry turns a pale brown colour. Heat the butter in a frying pan and sauté the onion until lightly browned. Allow to cool.

Whisk the eggs in a mixing bowl and gradually add the milk and cream, beating after each addition. Add the cheese, salt, pepper and, last of all, the cool onions to the egg mixture. Pour this mixture into the pastry case. Bake for 25–30 minutes.

55 minutes to make
Good source of protein, vitamin A, B group vitamins, calcium

Welsh Rarebit

Serve poured over toast, mashed potatoes, baked potatoes or rice and green vegetables.

8oz/225g Cheddar cheese
3 tablespoons cream
salt and freshly ground black pepper to taste
½ teaspoon mild mustard
Worcestershire sauce (without anchovies) to taste

Melt the cheese in the top of a double boiler. Gradually add the cream, stirring the mixture constantly. Add the salt, pepper, mustard and Worcestershire sauce and continue to stir until the mixture is very smooth and very hot. Serve immediately.

15 minutes to make
Good source of protein, calcium

Wild Rice and Peas

Serve with a side salad.

2oz/55g butter or margarine
8 spring onions, thinly sliced
4oz/115g wild rice
4oz/115g white or brown long grain rice
1 pint/570ml vegetable stock or water
4oz/115g petits pois
salt and freshly ground black pepper to taste

Heat the butter in a deep saucepan and sauté the onions gently over a low heat.

Wash and drain the two measures of rice and stir them into the sauté. Then add the vegetable stock and stir the mixture over a high heat.

Add the petits pois, salt and pepper when the mixture has come to a simmer. Then stir well, cover the saucepan tightly and leave over a low heat until the liquid has been completely absorbed.

Serve immediately.

40 minutes to make
Good source of vitamin A, vitamin C

COLD DISHES

Curried Eggs

You can try some variations by adding 1 tablespoon chopped tarragon, or 1 clove garlic, or 1 tablespoon capers, or 2 tablespoons basil.

6 eggs
½ teaspoon curry powder
1 teaspoon green relish
1 teaspoon mild mustard
2 tablespoons mayonnaise
salt and freshly ground black pepper to taste

to serve:
lettuce

Hard-boil the eggs, then peel them and slice them in half lengthways.
   Scoop out the the yolks and place in a mixing bowl with the remaining ingredients. Blend thoroughly, then spoon this mixture back into the egg white halves. Serve on a bed of lettuce.

15 minutes to make
173 calories per serving
Good source of B group vitamins

Tomato and Potato Mousse

This makes a delicious savoury starter for a dinner party or a late night snack. You can be as elaborate as you like with the decoration (try small slivers of tomato and sprigs of dill, parsley, mint or basil), or serve with a small quantity of béchamel sauce.

2lb/910g tomatoes
1oz/25g sugar
salt and freshly ground black pepper to taste
1 tablespoon lemon juice
3 teaspoons agar-agar flakes (vegetable gelatine)
5fl.oz/140ml hot water
8oz/225g cold potato puree
½ pint/290ml double cream

Skin the tomatoes and remove the seeds. Press the tomatoes in a saucepan to squeeze out a little of their juice and begin to cook them to a puree.

Add the sugar, salt, pepper and lemon juice to the tomatoes and continue cooking. Meanwhile, dissolve the agar-agar in the hot water and then add it to the tomatoes. Simmer for 2–3 minutes.

Add the potato puree to the tomato and gently fold together. Remove the mixture from the heat and allow it to cool. Taste it at this point, and add more seasoning if desired.

Lightly whip the cream and, when the puree is cool, blend the cream in with it. Pour the mixture into a lightly buttered 1 pint/570ml mould and allow to chill until firm (1–1½ hours). To serve, carefully turn the mousse onto a colourful serving plate and serve immediately.

2 hours to make
Good source of vitamin A, vitamin C

Devilled Eggs

I learned to make these as a kid, and was always asked to make them whenever my parents had a dinner party.

6 eggs
5 tablespoons mayonnaise
1 tablespoon green relish
1 tablespoon mild mustard

for the garnish:
paprika or chopped gherkin
lettuce leaves (optional)

Hard-boil the eggs (about 10–12 minutes), then shell them and slice them in half lengthways.

Scoop out the yolks, mash, and combine them in a mixing bowl with all the other ingredients.

When blended thoroughly, spoon the mixture into the egg white halves. Garnish, and serve on a bed of lettuce.

20 minutes to make
Good source of protein, B group vitamins

Mexican Refried Beans

Used in many Mexican recipes, a great filling for tacos.

1lb/455g dried pinto beans, washed and drained
2 pints/1.1l water
2 medium onions, chopped
7fl.oz/205ml vegetable oil or 7oz/200g vegetable suet
salt and freshly ground black pepper to taste

Measure the beans and water into a large saucepan and place over a high heat. Bring the water to the boil, cover the pan, turn off the heat and let the beans soak for 1½ hours.

Add the onions to the beans. Bring the liquid to a boil again, then reduce the heat and simmer, covered, until the beans are very tender, for about 2½–3 hours. Replace any water that is lost through evaporation. (If you want to save time here, use a pressure cooker to cook the beans.)

When the beans are very soft, mash them up (or use a blender) and add the vegetable oil, salt and pepper. Serve hot and cold.

3 hours 45 minutes to make
Good source of protein, B group vitamins, potassium, iron

Pressed Egg and Tomato

8 eggs
2 tablespoons mayonnaise
1 iceberg lettuce
4 fresh tomatoes
2–3fl.oz/60–90ml French dressing

Place the eggs in boiling water for 10 minutes until they are hard-boiled. Peel them and mash them well together with the mayonnaise, then press the mashed eggs into a greased, tall, straight glass (½ pint/290ml size) and chill in the refrigerator for at least 30 minutes.

Shred the lettuce and arrange it on serving plates. Place the sliced tomatoes over the lettuce.

Take the chilled egg from the refrigerator and run a knife round the inside of the glass to loosen the egg. Tip it out carefully and cut ¾–1 inch/1.5–2.5cm slices from it.

Place the egg slices over the tomatoes and cover the salad with the dressing of your choice.

40 minutes to make
Good source of protein, vitamin A, vitamin C, iron

Stuffed Curried Eggs

Serve cold with salads.

10 eggs
8 tablespoons mayonnaise
1 tablespoon curry powder
2 teaspoons soy sauce
1 tablespoon relish
1 tablespoon chopped fresh parsley
salt and freshly ground black pepper to taste

Hard-boil the eggs for about 10 minutes in boiling water. Peel the eggs and slice them in half lengthways. Remove the yolks and put them in a mixing bowl.

Mix the remaining ingredients in with the egg yolks and beat the mixture well to make a smooth paste.

Stuff the egg whites generously with the mixture, so that the filling stands up in a little mound on top.

25 minutes to make
Good source of vitamin A, B group vitamins, iron

SALADS, DIPS & PÂTÉS

Beetroot and Celery Salad

1 egg
2 medium beetroot
3 sticks celery
4 tablespoons olive oil
2 tablespoons vinegar or lemon juice
salt and freshly ground black pepper to taste

garnish:
lettuce leaves
chopped chives (optional)

Hard-boil the egg, then peel and slice it. Wash the beetroot but leave the 'tail' attached. Boil rapidly for 45 minutes, until tender, then peel and chop into small cubes. Chop the celery.

Combine the vegetables in a wooden bowl, then mix the oil, vinegar, salt and pepper and pour the dressing over the salad.

Toss gently and serve on a bed of lettuce, topped with slices of hard-boiled egg and chopped chives.

50 minutes to make
Good source of B group vitamins, vitamin C

Beetroot and Onion Salad

Serve with cottage cheese and lettuce.

6 medium beetroot
3–4 bunches spring onions
5fl.oz/140ml sour cream
1 teaspoon mild mustard
1 tablespoon lemon juice
1 tablespoon freshly chopped parsley or dill
salt and freshly ground black pepper to taste

Wash the beetroot but leave the 'tail' attached. Boil rapidly for 45 minutes, until tender, then peel and cut into long, thin strips. Place the strips in a mixing bowl.

Trim and thinly slice the spring onions and add them to the beetroot. Stir well.

Mix together the sour cream, mustard, lemon juice and seasoning in a jug, and pour it over the onion and beetroot mixture. Stir well and serve immediately or allow to chill.

50 minutes to make
Good source of vitamin A, vitamin C

Cabbage and Caraway Seed Salad

It helps to have a food processor for this recipe to make sure the cabbage is very finely shredded.

1 small white cabbage (12oz–1lb/340–455g), shredded
½ small onion, finely chopped
2 tablespoons lemon juice
5fl.oz/140ml mayonnaise
1 tablespoon caraway seeds
salt to taste

Mix all the ingredients together in a large salad bowl. Sprinkle with the salt and serve immediately.

10 minutes to make
Good source of vitamin C

Caesar Salad

1 clove garlic, crushed
1 teaspoon mild mustard
1 tablespoon lemon juice
1 tablespoon vinegar
4 tablespoons olive oil
1 egg
2 tablespoons grated Parmesan cheese
salt and freshly ground black pepper to taste
1 crisp lettuce
2 tomatoes, quartered (optional)
1 teaspoon capers (optional)

Rub the garlic around the inside of a large wooden bowl for flavour. Then mix the garlic with the mustard, lemon juice, vinegar, oil and egg in a jug. Whisk together. Add the cheese, salt and pepper, and whisk again.

Break the lettuce into the bowl, and add the tomatoes and capers if desired. Pour the dressing over the salad and mix well.

15 minutes to make
Good source of vitamin A, B group vitamins, vitamin C

Celeriac Salad

A simple but classic salad for that gourmet touch, great as a side dish at dinner parties. Do make sure that the celeriac is tossed in the dressing as soon as possible, or it will discolour.

1lb/455g celeriac roots
5fl.oz/140ml mayonnaise
1 tablespoon lemon juice
1 teaspoon mild mustard

Peel and wash the celeriac roots. Cut into very thin, almost transparent, strips or shred the roots coarsely. Mix the mayonnaise, lemon juice and mustard together in a serving bowl. Add the shredded celeriac and stir very well. Serve immediately or chill.

10 minutes to make

Cheese and Caper Dip

Try slivers of carrot, small stems of cauliflower, spring onions or other raw vegetables with this dip, or use with potato crisps or corn chips as a party dip.

4oz/115g cottage cheese
2 tablespoons chopped capers
1 teaspoon caraway seeds
4 tablespoons sour cream
1 tablespoon diced onion or spring onion
freshly ground black pepper to taste

In a mixing bowl combine all the ingredients and mix with a fork until everything is very well distributed. If the mixture is too thick for dipping, add a little milk.

Transfer into a pretty bowl and serve.

5 minutes to make

Celery and Rice Salad

Serve as a stuffing for avocados or tomatoes, or on a bed of lettuce with a sprinkling of sesame seeds. The mayonnaise needs to be quite thin – if it isn't, mix in 1–2 tablespoons of natural yoghurt or sunflower oil.

3 spring onions, chopped
6 sticks celery, chopped
5fl.oz/140ml mayonnaise
12oz/340g cooked rice
1 tablespoon chopped pickle or relish
1 tablespoon lemon juice
salt and freshly ground black pepper to taste

Mix all the ingredients together in a large bowl and serve.

10 minutes to make
Good source of vitamin A, vitamin C

Chef's Salad

A meal in itself – great when friends come round for lunch!

2 large crisp lettuces
8oz/225g Cheddar cheese, sliced or cubed
4 medium tomatoes, quartered
6 slices vegetable luncheon 'meat' in long strips

for the dressing:
1 tablespoon vinegar
1 tablespoon lemon juice
6 tablespoons vegetable oil or olive oil
salt to taste
1 teaspoon mild mustard
1 clove garlic, crushed
1 tablespoon chopped chives
1 tablespoon chopped parsley

Wash and thoroughly dry the lettuces and break them into small pieces. Place in a large wooden bowl. Add the cheese, tomatoes and luncheon 'meat' to the lettuce. Mix the dressing ingredients together in a jug. Beat well and pour over the salad. Toss, and serve immediately.

10 minutes to make
Good source of vitamin A, vitamin C, calcium

Chick Pea Salad

Chick peas are amongst the most delicious of legumes, with a distinct nutty flavour. If cooking them yourself, do make sure that they are very soft before using them – you should be able to squash them onto the roof of your mouth with your tongue.

1lb/455g cooked or tinned chick peas
6 sticks celery, trimmed and chopped
5fl.oz/140ml mayonnaise
2 tablespoons lemon juice
1 clove garlic, crushed
2 tablespoons chopped fresh parsley
1 tablespoon chopped onion or chives or spring onion
salt and freshly ground black pepper to taste
1 lettuce

Mix the chick peas and celery together. In a small bowl combine the mayonnaise with the lemon juice, garlic, parsley and onion. Season to taste. Stir the dressing into the chick peas and celery.

Wash the lettuce and line a salad bowl with the leaves. Pile the chick pea salad into the centre and serve immediately.

10 minutes to make
Good source of protein, vitamin A, B group vitamins, vitamin C

Coleslaw

½ head red or green or white cabbage, shredded
1 carrot, shredded
2fl.oz/60ml lemon juice
4fl.oz/120ml vegetable oil
salt and freshly ground black pepper to taste

Mix the cabbage and carrot together in a large bowl.

Stir the remaining ingredients together in a jug and pour the dressing over the salad. Stir very well and serve immediately or chill for 30–60 minutes.

10 minutes to make – unchilled
Good source of vitamin A, vitamin C

Cucumber Salad

1 large cucumber
1 tablespoon cooking salt
8fl.oz/230ml sour cream
1 tablespoon chopped chives or chopped onion
1 tablespoon lemon juice
3–6 sprigs fresh dill weed, chopped
1 tablespoon freshly chopped parsley
salt and freshly ground black pepper to taste

Peel and cube the cucumber. Place in a colander, cover it with the salt and leave for 30 minutes. The cucumber will 'sweat' off some of its excess juice.

Mix all the ingredients together in a large salad bowl and serve immediately, or chill for about 1 hour.

35 minutes to make – unchilled

gg and Potato Salad

2 eggs
1½lb/680g potatoes
2 tablespoons chopped onion or chopped chives or
  chopped spring onion
1 teaspoon mild mustard
1 tablespoon lemon juice or vinegar
5fl.oz/140ml mayonnaise
salt and freshly ground black pepper to taste

Hard-boil the eggs for 10–12 minutes. Allow them to cool, then peel and chop them.

Peel the potatoes and boil or steam them until tender. Allow them to cool, then cut them into small chunks.

Mix the chopped onion with the eggs and potato in a large bowl. Stir the remaining ingredients together in a small bowl, then gently mix into the salad. Serve immediately, or chill briefly first.

0 minutes to make – unchilled
Good source of vitamin C, potassium

Egg and Cheese Salad

This is a creative variation on an old favourite, and it tastes quite unlike any ordinary egg and cheese salad you've ever had before!

6 eggs
8oz/225g Swiss cheese
8fl.oz/230ml sour cream
1 tablespoon lemon juice
1½ teaspoons mild mustard
1 teaspoon horseradish sauce
pinch cumin seed
salt and freshly ground black pepper to taste

to serve:
1 lettuce
1 bunch watercress
4 tomatoes, sliced

Hard-boil the eggs for 10–12 minutes. Allow them to cool, then peel and chop them and place in a salad bowl.

Cut the cheese into small cubes and add to the eggs in the salad bowl.

Mix all the remaining ingredients together except for the garnish, and then mix them with the egg and cheese. Season to taste.

Chill the mixture, or serve immediately on a bed of lettuce surrounded by watercress and tomatoes.

25 minutes to make – unchilled
Good source of protein, vitamin A, B group vitamins, calcium

Four Seasons Salad

6oz/170g carrots, shredded
6oz/170g cucumber, chopped or sliced
6 sticks celery, finely chopped
1 bunch spring onions, finely chopped
to serve:
1 lettuce
5fl.oz/140ml mayonnaise or French dressing

Mix all the vegetables together in a large salad bowl. Serve with mayonnaise or French dressing on a bed of lettuce.

10 minutes to make
Good source of vitamin A, B group vitamins, vitamin C

Egg Salad Sandwich Spread

Use this spread in sandwiches, on crackers, as a filling for baked potatoes, in a salad or to fill an avocado.

3 eggs
2 sticks celery
1 tablespoon green relish or chopped pickle
4 tablespoons mayonnaise
1 tablespoon mild mustard

Hard-boil the eggs (for about 10–12 minutes). Allow them to cool, then peel and chop them finely.

Chop the celery finely. Combine the eggs and celery in a mixing bowl.

Add the green relish, mayonnaise and mustard and mix well.

15 minutes to make
Good source of B group vitamins

German Potato Salad

Serve with a selection of other salads, or chill and serve in small portions for packed lunches or picnics.

4 large potatoes, cubed
1 teaspoon mild mustard
5fl.oz/140ml sour cream
1 tablespoon white wine vinegar
2 tablespoons mayonnaise
salt and freshly ground black pepper to taste

Boil or steam the potatoes until they are just tender but don't fall apart. Allow them to cool, then place in a large salad bowl.

Mix the remaining ingredients together in a jug. Pour this sauce over the cooled potatoes, and stir gently until the potatoes are well coated. Serve immediately.

30 minutes to make

Guacamole

This addictive Mexican dip/spread should be served with corn chips or toast – enough for 6–8 people.

2–3 large ripe avocados
3–4 tablespoons fresh lemon juice or lime juice (or more to taste)
1–2 × 4oz/115g tins green chillies in brine
½ clove garlic, crushed (optional)
salt to taste

Slice the avocados in half lengthways and remove the stones. Scoop out the avocado pulp and mash it in a mixing bowl. Pour the lemon juice over the mashed avocado.

Drain and finely chop the chillies and garlic, if desired. Add them, with the salt, to the avocado. Stir the mixture very well to make a smooth paste.

15 minutes to make
Good source of vitamin A, vitamin C

Lemon Coleslaw

1lb/455g white cabbage
juice of ½ lemon
4–5 tablespoons oil
salt to taste

Shred the cabbage and place it in a large salad bowl.

Mix the remaining ingredients together and pour them over the cabbage. Let the cabbage absorb the dressing for at least 30 minutes before serving.

10 minutes to make
Good source of vitamin C

Hummus

1lb/455g cooked chick peas
2fl.oz/60ml water
3fl.oz/90ml lemon juice
4 cloves garlic, finely chopped
½ teaspoon salt
3 tablespoons tahini
2 tablespoons fresh parsley, chopped
3 tablespoons olive oil

Place all ingredients in a blender or food processor and puree to a fine consistency, adding a little more liquid as necessary to make a smooth, light paste. Serve immediately with salad and pitta bread.

5 minutes to make
Good source of iron

Lemon Rice Salad

 2 tablespoons chopped fresh parsley
 1 tablespoon chopped onion
 12oz/340g cooked rice
 2 tablespoons lemon juice
 4 tablespoons olive oil

 to serve:
 lettuce

Mix all the ingredients together and serve on a bed of lettuce.

5 minutes to make

Moroccan Carrot Salad

 3oz/85g currants
 4 seedless oranges
 1lb/455g carrots, grated
 1 medium onion, finely chopped
 1oz/25g walnuts, finely chopped
 ¼ teaspoon dried red pepper or paprika or cayenne
 3 tablespoons olive oil
 juice of 1 lemon
 salt and freshly ground black pepper to taste

Measure the currants into a small bowl and cover them with warm water. Leave them to soak for 10 minutes.

Peel and thinly slice the oranges. Mix these and all the remaining ingredients together in a large salad bowl and toss gently together.

Drain the currants and add them to the salad. Stir well and chill the salad for at least 30 minutes before serving.

45 minutes to make
Good source of vitamin A, B group vitamins, vitamin C, potassium

Potato Salad Vinaigrette

8 medium potatoes
4 tablespoons vinegar
6 tablespoons olive oil
1 tablespoon chopped chives
2 tablespoons chopped fresh parsley
1 sprig tarragon, chopped
salt and freshly ground black pepper to taste

Peel the potatoes and cube them. Boil, covered, for about 15 minutes until they are tender but not crumbling. Place them, still hot, in a large salad bowl.

Mix the remaining ingredients together in a jug, season to taste and pour over the potatoes. Stir gently and serve warm.

20 minutes to make
Good source of B group vitamins, vitamin C, potassium

Potato Salad and Mayonnaise

Serve with a selection of salads, a quiche, or a barbecue.

1½lb/680g potatoes
1 tablespoon chopped onion
6 sticks celery, chopped
salt and freshly ground black pepper to taste
5fl.oz/140ml mayonnaise
1 tablespoon lemon juice

Peel and chop the potatoes, then steam or boil them until just tender. Drain and allow them to cool.

Mix the onion and celery together in a large salad bowl. Stir the remaining ingredients together in a small bowl. Add the cooled potatoes and the dressing to the salad bowl and stir gently. Serve immediately.

30 minutes to make
Good source of vitamin C

New Potato Salad

1lb/455g new potatoes
4 heaped tablespoons thin mayonnaise
1 tablespoon finely chopped celery
1 tablespoon chopped pickle or relish
1–2 tablespoons natural yoghurt or sunflower oil
salt and freshly ground black pepper to taste

for the garnish:
2 tablespoons chopped fresh parsley

Scrub the new potatoes (do not peel) and boil or steam them for about 15 minutes until tender. Drain, allow to cool then cut into quarters. Place the cooled potatoes in a large salad bowl.

In a separate bowl, mix the mayonnaise, celery, pickle and yoghurt or sunflower oil. Season to taste. Add this to the potatoes and stir gently until the potatoes are well coated.

Top the salad with the chopped parsley and serve immediately, or chill and serve with other salads.

25 minutes to make – unchilled
Good source of vitamin C

Noodle Salad

8oz/225g noodles, uncooked weight
8oz/225g red cabbage, shredded
6oz/170g mushrooms, sliced
½ large cucumber or 1 small cucumber, sliced
6 tablespoons olive oil
6 tablespoons red wine vinegar
salt and freshly ground black pepper to taste

Cook the noodles and divide them into three portions. Place one portion in a large salad bowl.

Spread the shredded cabbage over these noodles. Place another portion of the cooked noodles over the cabbage.

Spread the sliced mushrooms over the noodles. Place the third portion of cooked noodles over the mushrooms. Top the salad with the cucumber.

Mix the oil, vinegar, salt and pepper together and pour over the salad. Do not toss. Serve after it has stood for 30 minutes.

50 minutes to make
Good source of B group vitamins, vitamin C

Raw Mushroom Marinade

Serve with salads or over toast.

  8oz/225g mushrooms, sliced
  2 tablespoons olive oil
  2 tablespoons vegetable oil
  1½ tablespoons wine vinegar
  ½ tablespoon lemon juice
  2 tablespoons chopped fresh tarragon or oregano
  salt and freshly ground black pepper to taste

Put the mushrooms in a pretty salad bowl.

Mix the oils, vinegar and lemon juice together in a jug. Add the herbs, salt and pepper and stir well.

Pour the marinade over the mushrooms and leave, covered, in a cool place for 3–6 hours.

5 minutes to make – not including time to marinate
Good source of B group vitamins

Refried Bean Dip

Serve with crisps, corn chips or toast.

  1 × 4oz/115g tin green chillies in brine
  2oz/55g Cheddar cheese, grated
  1 small onion, chopped
  4 teaspoons ready bought taco sauce
  1lb/455g refried beans (either tinned or make your own: see page 51)

Drain and chop the chillies. Mix all the ingredients together in a saucepan and cook over a low heat until the cheese starts to melt. Serve immediately.

10 minutes to make
Good source of protein, vitamin C, calcium

Stilton Pâté

Serve with raw vegetables, crackers or toast.

4oz/115g Stilton cheese
2 tablespoons lemon juice
3oz/85g cream cheese
2 teaspoons chopped fresh chives
½ teaspoon paprika

Blend the Stilton, lemon juice and cream cheese together in a bowl.
Add the chives and the paprika. Blend well.
Keep chilled until ready to serve.

10 minutes to make

Spinach Salad

If you grew up hating the taste of spinach, this salad is a real eye-opener! Do make sure that the spinach is new and fresh (i.e. the leaves are not too deep green in colour, and don't feel tough or leathery).

8oz/225g fresh spinach
2 eggs
2 large tomatoes, chopped
1 mild onion, chopped
2 cloves garlic, crushed
3 tablespoons crumbled cooked vegetable 'bacon'
   (optional)
2 tablespoons lemon juice
1 tablespoon vinegar
3fl.oz/85ml olive oil
salt and freshly ground black pepper to taste

Trim and wash the spinach, then dry it using a clean tea towel. Tear or slice the spinach leaves and put them on one side.
Hard-boil the eggs in boiling water for 10 minutes, then peel and chop them.
Mix the eggs together with the remaining ingredients in a large salad bowl, and stir gently.
Add the torn spinach to the salad, toss it well and serve immediately.

20 minutes to make
Good source of vitamin A, B group vitamins, vitamin C, potassium

Tabouli Salad

12oz/340g cracked wheat (bulgur wheat)
1 pint 8fl.oz/800ml boiling water
3oz/85g scallions or spring onions
2–3 whole tomatoes
4 tablespoons chopped fresh parsley
2 tablespoons chopped fresh mint
juice of 1½ lemons
4–6fl.oz/120–180ml olive oil
pinch of ground allspice
salt and freshly ground black pepper to taste
1oz/25g pine nuts (optional)

Measure the cracked wheat into a large bowl and pour the boiling water over it. Stir well, and leave to sit for 15–20 minutes while you prepare the veget-ables.

Chop the scallions and finely chop the tomatoes. Add them with the parsley and mint to the cracked wheat, and stir well.

Pour the lemon juice and oil over the salad, sprinkle with the spice, seasoning and pine nuts and gently toss the salad.

Chill the tabouli for 1 hour before serving, to allow the flavours to blend.

1 hour 30 minutes to make – including chilling
Good source of vitamin A, vitamin C

Tomatoes Stuffed with Cottage Cheese and Basil

4 large tomatoes
8oz/225g cottage cheese
1oz/25g chopped fresh basil
3 tablespoons mayonnaise
freshly ground pepper to taste

for the garnish:
lettuce leaves

to serve:
French dressing

Slice the tops off the tomatoes and scoop out their insides. Sieve the pulp to remove the seeds.

Add the remaining ingredients to the pulp, and mix them all together.

Spoon this mixture back into the tomato shells, and serve on a bed of lettuce with French dressing.

10 minutes to make
Good source of vitamin A, vitamin C, calcium, iron

Watercress and Lettuce Salad

1 bunch watercress
1 large lettuce
4 tablespoons olive oil
2 tablespoons vinegar or lemon juice
salt and freshly ground black pepper to taste
1 tablespoon chopped onion
1 clove garlic, crushed
1 teaspoon mild mustard

Wash and trim the watercress and lettuce, and leave to drain.

Mix the remaining ingredients together in a jug. Coarsely chop the drained watercress and lettuce and place in a large salad bowl. Add the dressing, toss well and serve.

15 minutes to make

SOUPS AND BREAD

Avocado and Dill Soup

This is a cold soup, perfect for dinner parties or summer picnics. Chill it and serve garnished with a little chopped dill or chives.

2 large ripe avocados
8fl.oz/230ml sour cream
2 tablespoons finely chopped fresh dill
15fl.oz/430ml cold vegetable stock
1 teaspoon soy sauce
salt and freshly ground black pepper to taste
a little chopped dill or chives for garnish

Cut the avocados in half, extract the stones, scoop out the flesh and place it in a blender. Add the rest of the ingredients and blend for 1–2 minutes until smooth. Chill for 20 minutes, garnish and serve.

30 minutes to make
Good source of vitamin A, B group vitamins, potassium

Avocado and Green Chilli Soup

This is a spicy chilled soup – serve garnished with chopped chillies or fresh parsley. Serves 4-6 people.

2 ripe avocados
24fl.oz/690ml milk
1 × 4oz/115g tin green chillies in brine
1 medium onion, chopped
salt and freshly ground black pepper to taste
2 tablespoons lemon juice
2 tablespoons sherry
chopped chillies or fresh parsley for garnish

Cut the avocados in half, extract the stones, scoop out the flesh and puree in a blender. Add the remaining ingredients to the blender and puree until a very even consistency is reached.

Pour the mixture into a serving bowl, garnish and serve immediately. Alternatively, you can pour the soup into individual bowls and chill them.

30 minutes to make
Good source of vitamin A, B group vitamins, vitamin C, calcium

Bortsch Soup

This is my personal variation on the traditional rich Russian, peasan
soup. It can be served hot or cold.

  1 lb/455g beetroot
  2 medium potatoes (about 4oz/115g when mashed)
  1 medium onion, chopped
  2 tablespoons lemon juice
  salt and freshly ground black pepper to taste
  1 pint/570ml vegetable stock or water
  5fl.oz/140ml sour cream

  for the garnish:
  4 tablespoons freshly chopped chives or parsley
  sour cream (optional)

Cook the beetroot until tender, then peel and slice. Boil the potatoe
and mash them.
  Put the cooled beetroot, mashed potato, chopped onion and lemor
juice in a blender or food processor and puree. Add salt and pepper
vegetable stock and sour cream and puree for a further 1 minute.
  Place the soup in the fridge and chill for 1 hour, then pour into
individual serving dishes and sprinkle a little chopped chives o
parsley on top to garnish, follow with a dollop of sour cream if desired

1 hour 40 minutes to make – including chilling
Good source of vitamin A, B group vitamins, vitamin C, potassium

Broccoli Cream Soup

Another delicious cold soup, perfect for summer or winter, refreshing and nourishing.

1lb/455g broccoli
1 large onion
2 sticks celery
1 large carrot
2oz/55g macaroni
12fl.oz/340ml vegetable stock or water
salt and freshly ground black pepper to taste
8fl.oz/230ml single cream

for the garnish:
2fl.oz/60ml sour cream

Chop the broccoli, onion, celery and carrot into cubes, and simmer them with the macaroni in half the vegetable stock for 15 minutes. Then place in a blender and liquidize.

Add the seasoning, the remainder of the vegetable stock and the single cream, and blend again.

Pour into a cold bowl and place in the refrigerator to chill for 1 hour. Serve with a little sour cream in the middle of each individual bowl.

1 hour 20 minutes to make – including chilling
Good source of vitamin A, B group vitamins, vitamin C

Carrot Cream Soup

Carrots like you've never tasted them before! Smooth, rich and tasty this chilled soup should be served with a garnish of chopped parsley sprinkled on top.

12oz/340g carrots, finely chopped
1 medium onion, finely chopped
2 sticks celery, finely chopped
1oz/25g butter
1¼ pints/710ml vegetable stock or water
2oz/55g white rice
salt and freshly ground black pepper to taste
8fl.oz/230ml single cream

for the garnish:
4 tablespoons chopped fresh parsley

Sauté the carrots, onion and celery in the butter, stirring constantly for 10 minutes over a low heat. Then add the vegetable stock and rice and bring to a gentle boil.

Simmer, covered, for 20 minutes or until the carrots and rice are tender, then remove from the heat and allow to cool for 10 minutes. Season to taste.

Pour the soup and half the cream into a blender and puree until smooth.

Transfer the soup into a large serving dish and stir in the rest of the cream with a wooden spoon. Chill for 1 hour. Garnish with the parsley and serve.

1 hour 45 minutes to make – including chilling
Good source of vitamin A, vitamin C

Corn Bread Mexican Style

Serve warm with butter or margarine.

2 eggs
4 tablespoons vegetable oil
2 × 4oz/115g tins green chillies in brine
4 medium ears sweetcorn or 1x12oz/340g tin sweetcorn, drained
4fl.oz/120ml sour cream
6oz/170g corn meal
2 ½ teaspoons baking powder
8oz/225g Cheddar cheese, grated

Pre-heat the oven to 350°F/180°C (Gas Mark 4) and lightly grease and flour an 8 inch/20cm round baking tin. Beat the eggs and oil together in a large bowl until they are well blended.

Drain and chop the chillies and trim the corn away from the cob. Add the chillies, sweetcorn and sour cream to the egg and oil mixture. Stir well.

Mix the corn meal and baking powder together and add to the batter. Add most of the cheese to the batter, but save enough to sprinkle on top.

Give the batter a very good stir and pour it into the baking tin. Sprinkle the remainder of the cheese on top and bake for 35–40 minutes, until a knife or piece of raw spaghetti inserted into it comes out clean.

1 hour 15 minutes to make
Good source of protein, vitamin A, B group vitamins, calcium

Corn Bread

This tasty bread can be served hot or cold, and is great with soups and salads.

2oz/55g self-raising flour
8oz/225g corn meal
½ teaspoon salt
½ teaspoon sugar
¾ teaspoon baking powder
3 eggs
12fl.oz/340ml milk
3oz/85g butter or margarine

Pre-heat the oven to 400°F/200°C (Gas Mark 6) and grease an 8 inch/ 20cm square baking tin. Mix the dry ingredients together in a mixing bowl.

Beat the eggs and milk together, pour into the dry mix and stir thoroughly.

Melt the butter and pour it over the mixture. Stir well.

Pour into the prepared tin and bake for 20 minutes.

30 minutes to make
Good source of vitamin A, B group vitamins, calcium

ream of Celery Soup

light and creamy soup, superb for a quick, nourishing snack.

1½oz/45g butter or margarine
8 sticks celery
1 tablespoon plain flour
1 pint/570ml milk
salt and freshly ground black pepper to taste
½ pint/290ml single cream

Ieat the butter in a large saucepan, then chop the celery into cubes
nd add to the pan. Stir over a medium heat for 5 minutes until the
elery becomes translucent.

Sprinkle the flour over the celery, then gradually add the milk and
easonings. Bring to the boil, stirring constantly, then simmer over a
ow heat for about 20 minutes. Puree the soup. Finally stir in the cream
nd gently reheat before serving.

5 minutes to make
ood source of protein, vitamin A, B group vitamins, calcium

Cream of Tomato Soup

Freshness is the essence of this soup, since it must be served as soon as it has been made. You've never tasted tomato soup so good!

1½ lb/680g ripe tomatoes, quartered
1 large onion, chopped
2 sticks celery, chopped
8 tablespoons vegetable stock or water
1oz/25g butter or margarine
¾oz/20g plain flour
1 pint/570ml milk
8 tablespoons double cream
salt and freshly ground black pepper to taste

Place the vegetables and stock in a large saucepan and simmer them gently for about 15 minutes, until very soft. Then either sieve the mixture, or puree in a blender and sieve afterwards to remove any pulp or seeds.

Melt the butter in a saucepan. Sprinkle the flour over the butter and whisk together until a very smooth paste is formed. Heat the milk and gradually add it to the paste, beating after each addition to make smooth sauce. Simmer gently for 4–5 minutes.

Add the cream and seasoning to the sauce and, just before serving, combine the sauce with the pureed vegetables and mix thoroughly. Serve immediately, otherwise the soup may separate or curdle.

40 minutes to make
Good source of vitamin A, vitamin C, calcium

French Carrot Soup

A delightful variation on a traditional favourite, this soup can be served hot, but may also be chilled and served cold with a spoonful of double cream stirred into each serving. For 4–6 people.

2oz/55g butter or margarine
1 large onion, chopped
2 cloves garlic, crushed
2 medium potatoes, chopped
1lb/455g carrots, shredded
1½ pints/860ml vegetable stock or water
1 teaspoon sugar
¼ teaspoon ground nutmeg
salt and freshly ground black pepper to taste
4 teaspoons double cream (optional for cold soup)

Melt the butter in a large saucepan and sauté the onion and garlic in it. Add the potatoes and carrots and stir-fry for 4–5 minutes. Then add the vegetable stock, cover the pan and simmer for 30 minutes until the vegetables are tender.

Puree the vegetables in a blender. Return them to the saucepan and add the sugar, nutmeg, salt and pepper. Stir well. Add a little extra vegetable stock or water if you want a thinner soup.

Serve the soup hot by bringing it back to a simmer when required. Alternatively, chill in the refrigerator.

50 minutes to make
Good source of vitamin A, B group vitamins, vitamin C, potassium

Delicious Watercress Soup

A hot soup for those misty autumn days, best served garnished with chives.

> 2oz/55g butter or margarine
> 2 medium onions, chopped
> 1 clove garlic, crushed
> 2 medium potatoes, cubed
> 2 bunches watercress, chopped
> 1½ pints/860ml vegetable stock or water
> salt and freshly ground black pepper to taste
> 12fl.oz/340ml milk
> 4fl.oz/120ml single cream
> 2 egg yolks, beaten
>
> for the garnish (optional):
> chives

Heat the butter in a large saucepan and lightly fry the onions and garlic for 2–3 minutes. Then add the potatoes and watercress and sauté them gently for 5 minutes, covered.

Add the vegetable stock to the pan, cover and leave to simmer for 15 minutes. Cool, and puree in a blender.

Pour the mixture back into the pan and add the seasoning. Mix in the milk, cream and egg yolks, heat gently for a few minutes to cook the egg yolks, then serve.

1 hour to make
Good source of vitamin A, vitamin C

Gazpacho

A simple, quick and delicious cold soup, this is my version of the traditional Spanish soup which is best eaten with fresh, crusty bread. Add more garlic if you can take it!

1 lb/455g ripe tomatoes
1 green pepper
1 cucumber
1 medium onion
1 clove garlic, crushed
1 egg
2 tablespoons/30ml wine vinegar or lemon juice
4 tablespoons olive oil
8fl.oz/230ml tomato juice
salt and freshly ground black pepper to taste

Skin the tomatoes by plunging them into boiling water, leave them for 1-2 minutes, then plunge them into cold water and peel off the skins. Then place them in a blender.

Remove the seeds from the pepper, chop it coarsely and add to the tomatoes.

Peel and chop the cucumber and onion, and add, with the garlic and egg, to the ingredients in the blender.

Measure the remaining ingredients into the blender. Cover and liquidize thoroughly. Add a little cold water to thin the mixture if necessary. Pour the soup into a chilled bowl and serve immediately.

10 minutes to make
Good source of vitamin A, vitamin C

Lentil Soup

A gorgeous, nourishing soup for the thick of winter, makes enough fo
4–6 people.

> 1 medium onion, chopped
> 2 tablespoons vegetable oil
> 1 clove garlic, crushed
> 6oz/170g carrots, chopped
> 2 sticks celery, chopped
> 4oz/115g lentils
> 1 bay leaf
> 1 tablespoon freshly chopped parsley
> salt and freshly ground black pepper to taste
> 1½ pints/860ml vegetable stock or water

Heat the oil in a very large saucepan and gently sauté the garlic an
onion. Add the carrots and celery and cook, stirring frequently, for 1
minutes.

Wash the lentils twice in cold water. Drain them and add to the par
Add the bay leaf, parsley, salt and pepper and stir well.

Pour in the vegetable stock, cover the pan and simmer the soup fo
1½ hours, until the lentils are very soft. Add a little extra stock or wate
if necessary.

1 hour 45 minutes to make
Good source of vitamin A, vitamin C

Herb Bread

1 long stick French bread
3oz/85g butter or margarine
4 teaspoons chopped fresh parsley
3 teaspoons chopped fresh basil or oregano or other fresh herbs

Pre-heat the oven to 350°F/180°C (Gas Mark 4). Slice the French stick along its length, but don't cut all the way through.

Melt the butter in a small pan and stir in the herbs. Brush this mixture all along the inside of each cut in the bread until it is all used up.

Wrap the whole French stick in foil and bake for 10 minutes. Serve immediately.

15 minutes to make

Irish Brown Bread

1lb/455g wholewheat flour
8oz/225g all-purpose white flour
2oz/55g rolled oats
1 teaspoon salt
1½ teaspoons bicarbonate of soda
15fl.oz/430ml buttermilk

Pre-heat the oven to 425°F/220°C (Gas Mark 7) and lightly grease a baking tray. Mix all the dry ingredients together in a large mixing bowl.

Make a well in the centre of this mixture and add enough buttermilk to make a soft dough. Mix the dough using a wooden spoon at first, then your hands.

Form the dough into one large or four small balls and flatten to 2 inches/5cm thick on the baking tray. Slice a cross in the top of each flattened loaf to a depth of ¾ inch/2cm. The cross should mark nearly the whole surface of the loaf.

Bake for 25 minutes, then reduce the oven temperature to 350°F/180°C (Gas Mark 4) and bake for a further 10 minutes. Place on a wire rack until cool.

50 minutes to make
Good source of protein, B group vitamins, calcium

Minestrone

Another all-time favourite, this soup takes a little time to prepare, but it's well worth it. Served with a green salad and crusty bread, it makes a meal on its own.

4oz/115g dried flageolet or haricot beans, soaked overnight
1 tablespoon olive oil
2 medium onions, chopped
2 cloves garlic, crushed
1 teaspoon dried parsley
1 teaspoon dried basil
2 courgettes, chopped
8oz/225g hard white cabbage, chopped
1 medium turnip, chopped
2 carrots, chopped
2 medium potatoes, chopped
3 sticks celery, chopped
4 tomatoes
1 tablespoon tomato paste
2 pints/1.1l water
4oz/115g macaroni
salt and freshly ground black pepper to taste
3oz/85g Parmesan cheese, grated

Drain the beans and rinse. Boil fast for 10 minutes, then turn down the heat and simmer gently for 50–60 minutes.

Heat the oil in a very large saucepan and sauté the onion and garlic. Add the herbs and continue to sauté.

Add the prepared vegetables to the saucepan and stir over a medium heat for about 5 minutes. Peel the tomatoes (plunge them into boiling water for 1–2 minutes, then into cold water, and remove the skins). Chop the tomatoes finely, removing the larger seeds. Add the tomatoes and the tomato paste to the vegetable mix and cover all with the water. Put a lid on the pan and simmer slowly for 45–60 minutes, until the vegetables are tender.

Add the macaroni and the cooked beans to the soup, with a little extra water if necessary, and cook for another 15 minutes, stirring well. Season with salt and pepper. Ladle into soup bowls and sprinkle with a little Parmesan cheese.

1 hour 30 minutes to make
Good source of vitamin A, B group vitamins, vitamin C, potassium

Parsley, Celery and Green Pea Soup

A beautiful and substantial soup. If you like a really thick texture, remove half of the soup halfway through cooking and puree in a blender, then return it to the pot.

  6oz/170g split green peas
  1oz/25g butter or margarine
  1 medium onion, chopped
  4 sticks celery, chopped
  2 carrots, chopped
  3 tablespoons chopped fresh parsley plus extra for garnish
  1 bay leaf
  1½–2 pints/860ml–1.1l vegetable stock or water
  salt and freshly ground black pepper to taste

Wash the peas and soak them either overnight in cold water or in hot water for 1 hour. Drain them and set to one side.

In a large saucepan, melt the butter and sauté the onion for 3–4 minutes, then add the celery and carrots and cook over a medium heat until lightly browned.

Add the drained peas, parsley and bay leaves. Mix well. Add the vegetable stock and stir well.

Cover the pan, bring to the boil, and simmer for 1–1½ hours until the peas are really tender. Stir the soup occasionally, and add more water or stock if desired. Season to taste and serve immediately, with a little chopped parsley sprinkled on top.

1 hour 45 minutes to make
Good source of protein, vitamin A, B group vitamins, vitamin C

Pasta Flageolet Soup

4oz/115g dried white beans (flageolet, haricot, or soy) soaked for several
hours or ready cooked
1 pint/570ml vegetable stock or water
3 sticks celery, chopped
1 medium onion, chopped
1 carrot, chopped
1 × 14oz/397g tin chopped tomatoes
salt and freshly ground black pepper to taste
1 teaspoon chopped fresh herbs (optional)
4oz/115g macaroni or broken spaghetti

Drain the beans, cover them with fresh water and bring to the boil.
Boil rapidly for 10 minutes, then cover the pan and simmer for 45–55
minutes or until tender. Drain the beans and reserve the stock.

Put the celery, onion and carrot in a large pan together with the
tomatoes, beans and ½ pint/290ml of the stock and stir well. Add the
salt and pepper and cook the mixture, covered, for a further 45
minutes.

Remove half of the mixture and puree in a blender, then return it to
the pan, stir well and leave it on the heat. At this point add the fresh
herbs and a little extra stock or water if desired.

In a separate pan cook the pasta in plenty of boiling, salted water
until tender, then drain and set aside.

Place a small serving of the cooked pasta in each of the serving
bowls, pour the hot soup over it and serve immediately.

2 hours 30 minutes to make
Good source of vitamin A, B group vitamins, vitamin C, potassium

Pizza Bread

A quick and tasty snack that young people love to make for themselves.

4 slices wholewheat bread
1–2 teaspoons oregano
1–2 cloves garlic, crushed
4 teaspoons olive oil
2 tablespoons tomato puree
8oz/225g Cheddar cheese, grated

Toast the bread lightly. Sprinkle with the oregano, garlic and oil. Spread the toast with the tomato puree, then add the cheese.

Place the pizzas under a hot grill until the cheese is bubbly and lightly golden. Serve immediately with a little extra oregano sprinkled on top if desired.

10 minutes to make
Good source of protein, B group vitamins, calcium

Potato and Carrot Bortsch

This variation on classic Bortsch may be served hot or cold.

> 12oz/340g beetroot
> 1 medium potato
> 4oz/115g carrots
> ½ pint/290ml water
> ½oz/15g butter or margarine
> 1 medium onion, finely chopped
> 1 stick celery, chopped
> 8oz/225g cabbage, shredded
> 1 × 14oz/397g tin chopped tomatoes
> 1 teaspoon dill weed to taste
> salt and freshly ground black pepper to taste
> 5fl.oz/140ml single cream
> ½ pint/290ml sour cream

Peel and finely dice the beetroot, potatoes and carrots and place them in a saucepan with the water. Bring to the boil and simmer, covered, until the vegetables are tender.

Melt the butter in a frying pan and sauté the onions, celery and cabbage.

Add the sauté to the vegetables in the saucepan. Add the tomatoes and dill weed and simmer the mixture for a further 15 minutes. Season to taste.

Just before serving, gradually add the single cream to the soup, stirring constantly. Place a dollop of sour cream in each serving bowl and ladle the soup on top.

45 minutes to make – unchilled
Good source of vitamin A, vitamin C, potassium

Sweetcorn Noodle Soup

Simple to make, delicious to eat, this hot soup is warming and filling on a winter's night.

2 pints/1.1l vegetable stock or water
4oz/115g noodles (ribbon or flat, broken)
1lb/455g fresh sweetcorn kernels
3oz/85g celery, chopped
2 hard-boiled eggs, chopped
½ teaspoon turmeric
salt and freshly ground black pepper to taste

Bring the vegetable stock to the boil. Add the noodles and the sweetcorn and boil for 5 minutes. Add the celery, chopped eggs and turmeric, stir well, reduce the heat and cook for a further 10 minutes. Serve immediately.

25 minutes to make
Good source of vitamin A

Turnip, Carrot and Split-Pea Soup

A real country soup, best eaten with lashings of hot buttered brown bread.

  6oz/170g split dried peas
  1oz/25g butter or margarine
  1 medium onion, chopped
  6oz/170g carrots, chopped
  6oz/170g turnip, chopped
  1–1½ pints/570–860ml vegetable stock or water
  salt and freshly ground black pepper to taste

Wash the peas and soak them overnight in cold water, or in hot water for 1 hour. Drain them and set to one side.

Heat the butter in a saucepan and sauté the onion until light brown. Add the carrots and turnip and continue cooking for 5 minutes. Add the peas and the vegetable stock, and stir well.

Cover the pan, bring to the boil and simmer for 1–1½ hours until the peas are really tender. Stir the soup occasionally and add a little water if necessary. Season to taste, and serve.

2 hours to make
Good source of vitamin A, vitamin C

Vegetable Soup

Everyone has their own favourite vegetable soup, and this is mine – try it and it could become yours too! Serves plenty.

2 tablespoons vegetable oil
1 large onion, chopped
2 leeks, sliced
3 sticks celery, chopped
1 clove garlic, crushed
4 medium carrots, sliced
8oz/225g cabbage, shredded
2 medium potatoes, chopped
1 teaspoon chopped fresh thyme
1 teaspoon chopped fresh rosemary
2 tablespoons chopped fresh parsley
1½ pints/860ml vegetable stock or water (1 pint/570ml
    if using tinned tomatoes)
8 medium tomatoes or 1 × 14oz/397g tin chopped
tomatoes
salt and freshly ground black pepper to taste

Heat the oil in a large saucepan and sauté the onion, leeks, celery and garlic for 5 minutes.

Add the carrots, cabbage and potatoes and stir well. Add the herbs. Cover with vegetable stock and simmer, with the lid on, for about 1 hour. Stir occasionally, and add more liquid if necessary.

If you are using fresh tomatoes, sit them on top of the vegetables for a minute or two, until their skins peel away easily. Then stir the skinned tomatoes into the soup. If you are using tinned tomatoes, add to the soup and stir well.

Season the soup with salt and pepper and serve piping hot.

hour 15 minutes to make
Good source of protein, vitamin A, B group vitamins, vitamin C

Vichyssoise

An elegantly simple cold soup, stunning at dinner parties where
usually serve it garnished with chopped chives. In the winter you ca
serve it hot.

4 tablespoons vegetable oil
1 medium onion, chopped
4 leeks, thinly sliced
2 medium potatoes, chopped
1½ pints/860ml vegetable stock
½ pint/290ml cream
5fl.oz/140ml milk
2 tablespoons soy sauce (optional)
salt and freshly ground black pepper to taste

for the garnish:
chopped chives

Heat the oil in a large saucepan and sauté the onion, leeks and potatoe
for 5 minutes, until the onions are translucent.

Cover the vegetables with stock, and simmer them for about 15–2
minutes until the potatoes are tender.

Transfer the cooked vegetables and liquid to a blender and puree
slowly adding the cream, milk, soy sauce, salt and pepper.

Pour the soup into a serving tureen and chill for 1 hour. Serve with
garnish of chopped chives.

1 hour 30 minutes to make – including chilling
Good source of vitamin A, vitamin C

Wine and Vegetable Soup

An unusual and sophisticated soup, perfect for late evening parties or celebrations.

4 large potatoes
1½ pints/860ml vegetable stock or water
1oz/25g butter or margarine
1 clove garlic, crushed
1 large onion, chopped
2 sticks celery, chopped
2 carrots, chopped
2 teaspoons chopped fresh thyme and/or basil
1 tablespoon olive oil
4fl.oz/120ml white wine
1–2 tablespoons soy sauce, to taste

Peel and cube the potatoes and boil them in the stock for 15 minutes, until they are tender.

In a large saucepan, melt the butter and sauté the garlic and onion. Add the celery, carrots and herbs.

Add the olive oil, potatoes and stock. Stir well, cover and simmer for 20 minutes.

Pour in the wine and the soy sauce, stir again, cover and simmer for a further 20 minutes, adding extra vegetable stock or water if necessary. Serve piping hot.

1 hour to make
Good source of vitamin A, B group vitamins, vitamin C

Index

Aubergine Fritters 1
Avocado and Dill Soup 66
Avocado and Green Chilli
  Soup 67
Baked and Creamed Sweet
  Potatoes 2
Baked Steaklets 3
Bean Tacos 4
Beer Rarebit 5
Beetroot and Celery Salad
  46
Beetroot and Onion Salad
  47
Bortsch Soup 68
Broccoli Cream Soup 69
Burger Goulash 6
Burgers á la King 7
Burgers Chop Suey 8
Cabbage and Carraway
  Seed Salad 47
Caesar Salad 48
Carrot Cream Soup 70
Cauliflower Gratin 9
Celeriac Salad 48
Celery and Rice Salad 49
Cheddar Cheese Balls 10
Cheese and Caper Dip 49
Chef's Salad 50
Chick Pea Salad 51
Coleslaw 52
Corn Bread 72
Corn Bread Mexican Style
  71
Corn Fritters 10
Courgettes with Apples 12
Cream of Celery 11
Cream of Celery Soup 73
Cream of Tomato Soup 74
Cucumber Salad 52
Curried Eggs 40
Delicious Watercress Soup
  76
Devilled Eggs 42
Egg and Cheese Salad 54

Egg and Potato Salad 53
Egg Salad Sandwich
  Spread 55
Four Seasons Salad 55
French Carrot Soup 75
French Fried Vegetables 14
Fried Mozzarella 13
Gazpacho 77
German Potato Salad 56
Green Bean Savoury 16
Green Beans and
  Mushrooms in Sour
  Cream 15
Guacamole 56
Herb Bread 79
Hot Mozzarella Sandwich
  18
Hummus 57
Irish Brown Bread 79
Leeks Vinaigrette 17
Lemon Coleslaw 57
Lemon Rice Salad 58
Lentil Soup 78
Meatless Balls 19
Mexican Omelette 20
Mexican Refried Beans 43
Mexican Rarebit 20
Minestrone 80
Moroccan Carrot Salad 58
Mozzarella Croquettes 21
Mozzarella French Loaf 22
New Orleans Okra 23
New Potato Salad 60
Niçoise Green Beans 24
Noodle Salad 61
Noodles and Garlic 25
Noodles German Style 26
Omelette 27
Parsley, Celery and Green
  Pea Soup 81
Pasta Flageolet Soup 82
Pasta with Herbs 28
Pasties 29
Peas in Cream 30

Pizza Bread 83
Potato and Carrot Bortsch
  84
Potato Dumplings with
  Brown Butter 30
Potato Salad and
  Mayonnaise 59
Potato Salad
  Vinaigrette 59
Pressed Egg and Tomato 4
Quiche 38
Ratatouille 31
Raw Mushroom Marinade
  62
Refried Bean Dip 62
Sauerkraut and Veggy
  Dogs 32
Sausage Rolls 33
Simple Stuffed Mushrooms
  34
Sloppy Joes 35
Spinach Salad 63
Stilton Pâté 63
Stuffed and Broiled
  Mushrooms 36
Stuffed Curried Eggs 45
Sweetcorn Noodle Soup 85
Tabouli Salad 64
Tarragon and Herb Eggs 3
Tomato and Potato Mousse
  41
Tomatoes Stuffed with
  Cottage Cheese and Basil
  65
Turnip, Carrot and Split-
  Pea Soup 86
Vegetable Soup 87
Vichyssoise 88
Watercress and Lettuce
  Salad 65
Welsh Rarebit 39
Wild Rice and Peas 39
Wine and Vegetable Soup
  89